Sunset Soiree

A couplet here and there

Chandana Bardia

BookLeaf Publishing

India | USA | UK

Made with ❤ on the BookLeaf Publishing Platform

www.bookleafpub.in

www.bookleafpub.com

Dedication

To my family, for your love.
To my friends, for your inspiration.
To life's joys and sorrows, for shaping these words.
And to you, dear reader, for giving them a home.

Preface

Life moves in seasons, each carrying its own hues, light
and shadow,
spring and fall,
warmth and frigidity.
This collection is a journey through my mind with
changing nature and emotions, where colors whisper
stories, and time paints the soul in shifting shades.

These poems are an ode to fleeting moments—the amber
embrace of autumn, the chills of winter's white, the riot
of spring's vibrancies , and the revelry of summer's sun.
Just as the seasons change, so do we, finding beauty in
transition and meaning in impermanence.

I invite you to wander through these pages, to feel, to
reflect, and perhaps, to find glimpses of your own
journey woven into these verses.

Acknowledgements

I thank my family and friends
my mentor and every person who inspired me.

1. Ether

Ether, the emporium of dreams,
With constellations of wishes,
Is a muse to many, including me.

I ink the paper &paint with words;
Poetry comes alive, and
With this muse, I live every thought.

That's how beautiful the night is—
Without you, yet always with you.

2. Dawning skies

A mesh of dawning responsibilities,
Or a mesh of vulnerabilities,
A face as delicate as a flower
Facing the harsh fleeting winds,
A prelude to a stormy dream,
Of eyes buried deep in awaiting
Tomorrow, escape the reality.
Reality of the inescapable desires
Wanting to claim the brilliant hues
Of dusk that sultrily teased the fading sun.

3. Seamless love

There you peek in again,
with your satin seams and
sanguine blush,
splitting my sky
in hues of emotions,
striking the strings
of my heart.

From my breaths
the restless clouds form,
to fall, to drench, to love,
to bloom in effervescence.

With your touch,
you transmute me,
from winter's pleasing
Sun to spring's vibrancy.

There's music, stories,
and poems in my tiny

world of imagination, but
your reality bring seasons.

Now, I am an incarnation of love,
your love!

4. Alchemy

The long, endless winter ended
When alchemy of his touch
thawed the last snowflake of her heart,

Wrapping her in carnival colours,
splitting the sky wide open,
he showered ethereal songs of love.

Burning the soft words,
he packed away the colourless possessions, the breathless
regrets, apologies, and doubts.

An origami of being, he traced
and folded them into a
newfound stream of life.

Love found a new definition.

5. Silence

Silences swallowed the tears I couldn't speak,
his words, a haunting echo in the quiet.
Silence, a turned page, marked his absence,
a simple goodbye, a chasm now between us.
Silence, a heavy wait, unanswered apologies,
questions lost in the vast emptiness.
Silence consumed the love that beat within,
his heart, once mine, now still, no longer calling my
name—
A fading whisper.

6. Addiction

Neither day nor night,
the dusk wore a bright-hued visage,
with frills and fringes of sun rays.
It sultrily manoeuvred into the romantic night,
where love rested its limbs.

There, I waited, with my eyes on the watch,
for with the moon, you'll meet me.

7. When this is over

When this is over,
let's seek answers
and ask questions,

When I ask you,
Why did you leave me?
Don't let stars be
burdened,own up!

Why were promises
unkempt?
Don't let silence
be your weapon!

When you ask me,
Did you wait?
You'll find
your answer in
depth of my eyes!

8. Storm

The thinning night slipped through her cinnamon eyes,
which were deeper than Shakespeare's tragedies & held
more silence than words.

They traced contours of dreams reflected in his misty
eyes, which wore metaphor of a Neruda's sonnet.

Both of them defied & denied love.

9. Conversation

on my skin,
you paint glyphs,
you pin
stories of your desires,
you leave dreams
on my contour,
you #speak with your
touch, and imprint
a sigh.

I quiver with a moan,
and my sigh escapes with
a drop rolling down my cheeks.

10. Muse

Gossamer rays fell
upon the last
moments of dusk,
clinging to the poem
that remained trapped
in the day's realm.

A network of emotions,
much like mycelium,
became the muse as dusk transformed into night.

How delicate,
how intricate it felt,
only a lover knew.

11. Shadows

hold me again in your breaths,
I am cold holding your fragrance

kiss me again with your love,
I am frigid with your unthawed moments

contrive me again with your words,
I am algid with your broken metaphors

caress me again with your touch,
I am benumbed winter, without you.

12. Penumbra

Hold me in your love again,
I beseech you.
You were #penumbra;
be the light I seek.
I am cold,
keeping your breath warm.

Hold me in your kiss again,
I implore you.
You were the shadow,eclipsed;
be my moon.
I am a dream,living your euphoria alive.

13. Find me

Find me,
Find me in the backspaced verses,
Find me in chorus of heartbeats,
Find me in unspent emotions,

Find me in unvoiced words,
Find me in autumnal sojourn,
Find me in ink's sacrifice,

Find me in winter's silence,
Find me in dream's engagement,
Find me in you.

14. Looms

With looms of moonlight
woven in finery
of #exotic dreams
of love and passion,
with star- embellished arras,
with chrysanthemums and
sea breeze,
you and I,
together circle the
never ending story.
Then
the night seems like a paradise.

15. She

She who wears the crown,
Has many roles to play,
She who is mother, daughter,
Sister, wife, friend,
Is always a woman first;

She is always a woman first

One who is a realisation of dreams,
A custodian of tomorrow,
She rewrites destinies;

The crusader for eras,
with her pen, silence, and weapons she is a Renaissance;

The creator of the world,
she moulds, shapes, paints lives,
she is sculptor of today and tomorrow;

She is the goddess, the revered,

She knows to fight and forgive;
She is fire and ice;

She is Amrita, Savitri, Laxmi, Anna,
Sarojini, Durga, Saraswati,
she is you and me ..

16. Is she a dream?

"Who is she?"
"Bound by ties, she is a mother, daughter, wife"

No, she is the force,
architect of the future.
She is current, clay, & steel.
Creator, wielder, shaper.

"Who is she?"
"Defined by others?"

No. She is defined by herself.
Women—one word, many roles.

17. Thoughts of you

Did you have your morning
coffee thinking of me,
my lips felt the warmth.

Did you whisper a few
words of love, I felt the
breeze talking to my tresses.

Did you smile,
I saw the flowers bloom
in most vibrant hues.

18. Hold on

With a little love
that remains,
I hold on,
I clutch it tight,
braving all odds.
I will hold on.

Love never fades,
love's embers glow,
but emotions evolve
with storms that rage,
through shifting tides.

I will hold on!

19. Wordless Dawn

What should I write today?

The pain washes the ink away.
My thoughts feel burdened;
a goodbye did not end
an era of good times,
but it extinguished the hope
that once flickered within.
It was love, or perhaps connection,
but it was mine while it lasted.

20. Dusking Dreams

Behind the trail of flocculent dust,
the life of a city—or rather, life in a city—
gathers memories, seeking possibilities within them.
Darkness, in its quiet existence,
settled on the horizon,
and moonlight grew clearer.
In this, the lone face of a relentless poet smiled,
anticipating a rendezvous with the beloved.

The fluorescent billboards flashed,
a vibrant life in stark contrast
to the stillness of life in ink and paper.
It felt like a parallel universe,
existing within the poet's own.
But the disdain for the dark was camouflaged
by the glow of love.
Here, the poet saw the possibility of meeting the muse.

21. Hues

Rufescent rapture to invoke passion,
Verdant vitality to flourish
Amber Aurora for sunshine creativity
Sapphire serenity for calm retort,
Violaceous vibe for bond of love,
Amorousness of amethyst
To sing in strength and spirituality.
I paint you in hues of life !

22. Desirous Dwelling

he sky was busy,
spewing stories of love.
It scattered metaphors,
satiating the parched earth.
There, amidst the tales and analogies,
betwixt storm and rainbows,
under the shared umbrella,
two bodies entwined,
or rather, destined as one,
collided with the motion of oceans,
the emotion of barren parts within.
For months of monsoon,
for a season of desire,
deep within, they assured,
love was the catalyst.
But passion whispered a different track,
unbeknownst, porcelain skin
rested in lace's embrace,
sensual feet tracing the bed,
and thoughts laid bare.

They delved into each other.
The thunder rose again,
energies found endless release,
flowing freely in intimate encounters